Night Parables
Keys to Understanding Your Dreams

Humphrey Mtandwa
'I am Daniels'

Copyright @ Humphrey Mtandwa 2019

Edited by Phillip Kundeni Chidavaenzi

Typesetting by Royalty Books

Cover design by Ronny Israel

All rights reserved. No part of this publication may be reproduced, stored in a retrieval system, or transmitted in any form or by any means mechanical or electronic, photocopying or otherwise, without the prior permission of the author.

CONTENTS

Introduction i

Section 1

Stewardship 1
The Word 3
The Baker's Dream 4
12 Categories of Dreams 6
Understanding Your Dreams 10
Dream Cycle and Demonic Attacks 12
Power of Lucid Dreaming 12

Section 2

First Stage of Interpretation 15
Keys to Dream Interpretation 15
Unlocking Dreams that Include Others 16
Conclusion of First Stage 17
Final Stage of Interpretation 18
Examples of Dream Interpretation 19
22 Common Dreams 20

Section 3

Dream Directory 29
Numbers 29
Colour Chart 31
Animal Symbols 34
Insects 39
Buildings and Places 40
Rooms in a House 43
Directions 44
Weather 45
Body Parts 46

Other Symbols..47
Weapons and Objects..48
Clothing...49
Transport..50
People.. 53
Food Items..54

Section 4
Dreams and Warfare... 56
How to have Victory in Your Dreams...................... 58
Prayers of the Blood and Communion.................... 59
Weapons of Warfare in Dreams............................. 60
Conclusion.. 61

INTRODUCTION

EVERY symbol within a dream is important. I have learnt through years of experience that these symbols are not the final interpretations but just tools to help you unlock the meaning of the dream. A dog, in some dreams, is a symbol of a demonic spirit while in others it can symbolise an angelic helper. So when interpreting a dream, symbols are important but the key is application. The Spirit of God helps you understand each dream. The secret is to understand his personal dream language for you.

I have observed that some people do not even see the value of dreams. Are dreams important and do they still have importance in the present day church?

"And when they were departed, behold, the angel of the Lord appeared to Joseph in a dream, saying, Arise, and take the young child and his mother, and flee into Egypt, and remain there until I bring you word: for Herod will seek the young child to destroy him." **(Matthew 2 vs 13 NKJV)**

The importance of a message is measured by the method of communication used to transmit it. Effective communication is imperative and the best communicator is God because His communication ability transcends culture or tradition and there is nothing that can stop him from effectively transmitting a message.

When He decided to warn Joseph, the father of Jesus, of the danger that was coming, He chose something as simple as a dream. Dreams are night parables and it has been said that a parable is an earthly story with a heavenly meaning.

The Lord Jesus frequently used parables as a means of illustrating profound, divine truths. A dream carries pictures and information that you can relate to within your daily life. Parables are stories that you can easily remember. Jesus employed many graphic analogies using common things that would be familiar to everyone. It is no wonder, therefore, that he still employs dreams in our time to communicate with us. He often uses the same pictures we can relate with. If you look at the story of the Good Samaritan, for instance, you will realise that its value transcends time. The same value it had in Jesus' time can evolve to be the same value in our time.

SECTION 1

STEWARDSHIP:
KEY TO MASTERING YOUR DREAMS

"To those who listen to my teaching, more understanding will be given, and they will have an abundance of knowledge. But for those who are not listening, even what little understanding they have will be taken away from them." (Matthew 13 vs 22, NLT).

IF you are not faithful with the dreams or the visions the Lord gives you, they stop, but if you are faithful, they increase. If you are not faithful with the talents and gifts you are given, they stop, but if you are faithful, they increase with each day.

In one of his testimonies, Rick Joyner said there was a period he did not have dreams and he asked God why he no longer revealed Himself through dreams. Then the Lord told him it was because he had not been a good steward of the dreams he had received in the past. If you don't value something, you lose it. A relationship you don't put an effort into eventually dies. You can be surprised most prophetic people are dreamers and their dreams increase because of the value they put in them. Learn to always write down each encounter or instructions you receive in your dreams. Search out the meaning of your dream and revisit your journal often.

10 Keys to Increasing Your Dreams

1. Pray before you sleep asking God to visit you in your dreams. In the Jewish culture, they would invite God to visit them in their dreams because they understood the value of dreams.

2. Force yourself to wake up two or three times during the night. During a single night, a person can have more than one dream. This helps you remember all the dreams easily.

3. Don't immediately sleep after watching a movie. Pray for 30 minutes or more and read the Bible.

4. Write down or record your dreams. Because of technology, people normally use their phones now to record. Have audio recordings of your dreams and journal the interpretation as well.

5. Don't jump out of bed in the morning. Spend a few minutes meditating on your night and dreams. This allows you to retain all the dreams and emotions within the dreams.

6. Stewardship is the key for growth in EVERY area of our life! So if you want your dreams to grow, value them. What was the last dream you had and what instructions were in the dream? What was the interpretation?

7. The more you act on your dreams, the more they grow. Make sure you act on all instructions released to you through your dreams.

8. Always ask the Lord to speak to you and be attentive to His voice in your dreams.

9. Sometimes the Lord will tell you to steward an area that has NOTHING to do with the area you feel has no effect on you in any way.

10. What you value grows and what you neglect dies out.

The Word: Key to Understanding Your Dreams

The primary tool to interpretation is the word of God. It carries major symbols that we use for interpretation. Consider grass, for instance. In the Bible, it is a symbol of man. We see, *"My days are like a shadow that declineth; and I am withered like grass"* **(Psalms 102 Vs 11)**. The Bible also says, *"out of the mouth of two or three witnesses a testimony is* *confirmed" **(2 Cor. 13 vs 1)**. So, when looking for symbols in the Bible, there must be a least three scriptures that confirm. Our example of man as grass can also be seen in Psalms 104:14, Isaiah 37:27 and Job 5:25. Most of the symbols we use in interpretation are from the Word and that's the primary foundation of dream interpretation. Grass can also be a symbol of human life and its fragility. The scriptures are the foundation to build upon in understanding how God communicates.

The Baker's Dream

"When the chief baker saw that the interpretation was good, he said unto Joseph, I also was in my dream, and, behold, I had three wheat baskets on my head:" **(Gen 40 vs 16)**

Did you notice when the baker realised the interpretation to the cup bearer's dream was good, he also wanted an interpretation? That's how we apply symbols we have read in books. We use them directly, but when interpreting, the key is the Spirit of God.

The Colour Chart can be a good example. It can have five meanings for one colour. When you depend on God for your interpretation, He shows you which one among the choices is yours and how to apply it to your situation. On the Colour Chart, pink can mean a priest in prayer or a season of sacrifice in another dream or being feminine in yet another.

*"When the chief baker saw that the interpretation was good, he said unto Joseph, I also was in my dream, and, behold, I had three wheat baskets on my head: 17 And in the uppermost basket there was of all manner of bakemeats for Pharaoh; and the birds did eat them out of the basket upon my head." **(Gen. 40 vs 16-17)***

Note the interpretation...

*"And Joseph answered and said, This is the interpretation thereof: The three baskets are three days: 19 Yet within three days shall Pharaoh lift up thy head from off thee, and shall hang thee on a tree; and the birds shall eat thy flesh from off thee." **(Gen. 40 vs 18-19)**.*

The baker had three wheat baskets and each basket spoke of a day in the dream of the butler. Each branch symbolises a day as well. The baskets had bread meats inside and birds came and fed from the top basket. Some birds in dreams are demonic and they come as a symbol of the spirit of death. The butler's branches budded and it meant restoration and in the baker's case, the birds destroyed to show loss of life. Both dreams had a central theme. There would be a manifestation in three days.

Each dream had different symbols for days. And if the butler was also to die, there would have been a symbol of a worm eating the branches. Each dream carries specific instructions for the dreamer.

God's communication with us as men is creative beyond understanding and more far reaching in its scope than we can comprehend. He can reach every part of our life through the means of dreams if He so desires. It's your responsibility to learn how to interpret when He speaks for the Bible says it's the glory of God to conceal a thing but the honour of kings to search out a matter (Proverbs 25 vs 2).

12 Categories of Dreams

1. Dreams of Destiny and Calling
   These are dreams of discovery where one understands their call or purpose. Joseph is an example (Genesis 37 vs 5). At that moment he failed to see that the dream was not about his brothers bowing to him but him being the salvation of the world. Another "calling vision" was that of Samuel when the Lord called him. It was an encounter at night.

2. Dreams of Revelation of God's Word and Scriptures
   These are dreams where God reveals His will either through a specific scripture or revelation. My third and fourth books came to me in dreams. It can be a specific scripture that can be used to guide you in whatever you are doing

and when you receive such a revelation, meditate on that word until you have understanding of it. (2 Peter 1 vs 20-21).

3. Dreams of Edification and Exhortation
   Jacob saw the ladder of God and angels going up and down the ladder, coming to exhort and comfort him, assuring him that God would be with him. A word that brought strength was spoken (Genesis 28:12-17). Jesus also received strength when he saw angels in the Garden of Gethsemane before His death on the cross.

4. Dreams of Comfort
   Apostle Paul saw an angel in a vision of the night that encouraged him and reassured him they would not perish at sea (Acts 27 vs 23). These dreams come as encouragement in times of trouble.

5. Dreams of Direction
   When Joseph wanted to put away Mary his wife because she got pregnant before their marriage, an angel appeared to him in a dream and directed him on what to do. (Matthew 1 vs 20). Joseph also got an instruction to flee with his wife and child to Egypt (Mathew 2 vs 12-13).

6. Dreams of Correction

When King Nebuchadnezzar had a dream of the big tree that filled the whole world and failed to repent, he later on faced judgement because he did not follow through the instructions given by Daniel (Daniel 4:5-37).

7. Dreams of Instruction

Job 33 vs 14-17 tells us how God seals up instructions in us as we sleep as happened with Joseph the father of Jesus (Matthew 2:12-13). He was told where to go with the baby. Joseph was instructed in three different dreams on steps to take to ensure the safety of Jesus.

8. Dreams of Washing

To wash is a ritual in the Jewish culture, which is a symbol of separation from old life or sin. When you see yourself washing in a dream, it is a symbol of separation from sin or any form of weakness caused by sin. (Leviticus 14 vs 8-9).

9. Dreams of Warfare

These are at times attacks in dreams for those that have not mastered how to have victory in their dreams. In the Bible, we learn that the best way to prepare for war is through knowledge and training. An example of a dream of warfare is that when a man from Moab had a dream of Gideon winning the war (Judges 7 vs 13). These dreams usually come to reveal to you the battles you are fighting and strategies on how to win. It can be issues at work or family even or any place you where you relate with others.

10.   Dreams of Deliverance
Apostle Peter thought he was sleeping when an angel led him out of the prison after he had been caged by King Herod. These are not just dreams but a form of lucid dreaming that is induced by God to deliver you from the enemy's camp (Acts 12 vs 5-17).

11.   Dreams of Positioning
These dreams come to position you in God's will for your life. They can come to help you deal with emotions like the loss of a loved one, or even acceptance of something that will be coming. They deal more with emotions and your soulish side.

12.   Dreams of Inspiration (Creativity)
These dreams come to inspire you to exercise your creative abilities. You can read of how God inspired Bezaleel in Exodus 31.

The 12 dream categories may not be the only categories of dreams but I just used those for study purposes. Each dream carries a unique pattern, like a fingerprint. God's ability to communicate cannot be categorised, but most of man's dreams revolve around the 12 I highlighted. There are also three different sources of dreams, according to John Paul Jackson. But these sources can influence the 12 categories, like in dreams for deliverance, if it's a demonic dream, it can carry negative attacks where you see yourself being bitten by a snake or having sexual dreams. Each category is important to view through the lenses of the three sources of dreams. Dreams from the soul can be an expression of your desires rather than God's heart.

1. Dreams from God
2. Dreams from your soul/flesh
3. Demonic dreams

Understanding Your Dreams

Every individual has a unique dream pattern. You need to acquire the ability to understand your dreams or visions by understanding your dream pattern. The pattern can be colour or number symbols. When you learn your pattern, you can easily interpret your dreams.

Joseph's major dreams were about his family bowing to him. The common symbol was the number of his brothers, either shown as stars or haystacks. When the dream included the sun and the moon, that was further revelation. Was the dream just about him being above his brothers or it had greater significance? Later on we learnt it was not about him being ruler over his brothers but him being the salvation of the whole world.

The key symbol was "numbers" in all the dreams as an indicator of his brothers. When you look at the Number Chart and interpret Joseph's dream directly, you may fail to interpret it correctly. When you understand your pattern, it can have its own meaning like the number of stars and haystacks where a symbol of Joseph's brothers was used. To one person, white can mean happiness and to another, maybe death. The key to interpretation, therefore, is always the Spirit of God and you as the dreamer. The purpose of the directory is to give a framework but you need the Word of God as your primary tool for interpretation.

Most individuals can have a dream of a familiar person who is in trouble. Assuming that the dream is about that person is wrong because 95 percent of our dreams are about us as individuals. A familiar face in a dream can have meaning from the role they play in your life or just their social standing. Due to man's limited knowledge of the things of the Spirit, dreams often carry natural symbols that one can relate with.

A neighbour is supposed to be a friend in the natural but in dreams, they symbolise an enemy. When interpreting dreams, it's important to realise that the first place to understanding your dreams is to discover yourself through God's eyes.

Dream Cycle and Demonic Attacks

Most dreams repeat themselves because the dreamer would have ignored the message at the dream's first instance. Even dreams where one is attacked are repeated until you have victory in that area of attack. Many women, and even men, are tormented by dreams of a sexual nature. Such dreams come because of certain roots in one's life or foundations. A woman can be spiritually married and these sexual demons attack her because of the marital rights they have over her in the spirit. Even men can also be married off spiritually, but with men, it's usually a spirit of lust. But just because these are the common entry points of attack does not mean they are the only ones. These dreams repeat themselves because you, as the dreamer, would not have gained victory in that situation.

Other cyclic or recurring dreams keep happening because one would have missed the instruction being released in the dream. Not all repetitions in dreams are attacks, however. Some are messages one would have missed.

Power of Lucid Dreaming

After an attack in a dream, you can claim back your victory by getting back into your dream through meditation. Wake up during a dream, especially if you are being attacked, and meditate while awake on ways you can have victory. Stay awake for a while thinking on the dream and the desired outcome. Concentrate on the dream and fall asleep again. When you get back in the dream you can claim your victory. Even after you've lost a battle, go back and fight again. You will realise that you will pick up from where the dream ended.

SECTION 2

FIRST STAGE OF INTERPRETATION

Keys to Dream Interpretation

EACH dreamer has a unique dream pattern, so when you understand your dream pattern, it becomes easier to interpret your dreams. Remember, however, that interpretation primarily belongs to the Lord. You have to have the Holy Spirit to be able to understand and interpret your dreams. Dreams are inspired of God.

Unlocking Your Personal Dreams

- Most of your dreams will be about YOU!
- It is a common mistake most dreamers have to assume that the message is not personal but for others and miss the message God is sending them.
- When interpreting your own dream seek God's wisdom on how the dream applies to you personally.

- After interpretation, there are always instructions within the dream that have to be followed.
- Look closely and record all details in the dream also take not of the mood and your emotions within the dream.
- All details are important from your clothes to your emotions

Unlocking Dreams That May Include Others

- These dreams can involve the dreamer and even affect his environment. They have far-reaching impact so they must be approached carefully.
- These dreams are dependent on your responsibilities. The more responsibilities you have, the larger your sphere of influence and the more of these dreams you have.
- At times they may carry a message about the community you stay in or that you are sent to impact.
- The more you grow spiritually, the less personal your dreams become.

Conclusion of First Stage of Interpretation

There are two types of interpretations of dreams: those about the dreamer and those about others or dreamer's place of influence. The key is to identify which dream it is.

Second Stage of Dream Interpretation

- Break down the dream to form you can easily understand break it down to scenes if it's a large dream.
- Contextualising the dream put a topic or pick up the most important details.
- Ask yourself how serious is the dream? Maybe it's repeating itself or carries symbols you cannot ignore. Dreams that occur in one night can be centred on the same subject.

Questions to ask when interpreting your dream:
- Where are you in the dream?
- Are you observing?
- Are you participating?
- Are you the focus?
- Who is this dream about?
- What are the object, thoughts and emotions in the dream?
- Which person(s) is in your dream? What character trait or calling does the person represent to you? What does the person's name mean? What is their relation to you?
- What are the colours in the dream?
- Do certain numbers appear?

- What are your initial thoughts about what the dream pertains too?
- Questions, Questions, Questions???

Final Stage of Interpretation

Application is the final stage of dream interpretation. But how can someone apply what they have not fully understood? What is the dream saying and have you fully understood it? Make notes under the dream because a dream's meaning today may not be the same tomorrow. God can reveal more about the dream with time. A dream can reveal God's thoughts for you today but tomorrow, the same dream can reveal different thoughts.

Questions to ask in dream application
- If the application is for now or the future
- If there was an attack in the dream and if there is need to cancel the negative effects of the dream
- If there is a need to seed or give something do to secure your miracle
- If there is need to go on a fast
- James said faith without works is dead act on your dream and follow what the interpretation requires.
- Cancel anything negative the dream suggests.
- Prayer is major key in Dream application

- Ask for wisdom to act and fulfil one's dream

Examples of Dream Interpretation

Dream 1

I am not familiar with place that I was in but the person I remember was my friend. A snake appeared and started chasing my friend. It was a very scary dream because the snake managed to bite my friend.

1. Is the dream about the dreamer or the friend?
2. Who is the central character in the dream and what is the main focus?
3. Is the fact that the snake bit the friend and not the dreamer important?
4. What else is in the environment that's necessary to understanding the dream?
5. Is the name of the friend important?
6. What could be the application and how is the dreamer to respond?

Dream 2

I keep having the same dream where I find myself in my village. In this dream, I was working on the garden but it seemed as if I was just tired. I could not gather strength to continue working. When I sat down, I noticed I was carrying something on my back. It was a bag and it was grey in colour. I removed the bag from my back and felt revived and wanted to continue with the work.

1. Who is the dream about?
2. Why does the dreamer keep going to the village? Could there be something significant at the village?
3. Are there issues at the dreamer's village that may need attention?
4. Why was the dreamer in the garden?
5. Is there is importance attached to the colour of the bag?
6. Does the bag affect the dreamer from working in the garden?
7. Why where they revived?
8. Are there special prayers one should pray and what are those?

22 Common Dreams

1. Dreams in your village or foundational home (where you grew up)

   These dreams indicate there are issues that you have to deal with, dating back to your foundational home. It can be things that happened to your ancestors but which still affect you. Any time you see the house you grew up in or village, you're dealing with foundational issues.

2. Dreams of being bitten by snakes
   These are usually demonic attacks and when dealing with snakes in a dream, look at the colour and type of snake. A green snake can mean an attack on your source of provision or something that sustains you. A yellow snake can be symbol of blood related issues. A constrictor can be a spirit sent or limit you. Pay attention to detail.

3. Dreams of nudity or nakedness
   These dreams come to reveal areas of weakness with the need to produce transparency. Most areas of weakness become exposed and the most common dreams are of shame, while others are of transparency in your area of weakness. When exposed, those areas that could have been secret sins will not hold you back and you will grow more in the Lord. John Paul Jackson says these dreams usually occur during times of transition.

4. Dreams of spiders, cats and bats
   These three are some of the examples of witchcraft or occult systems. Depending with the dream and conditions within the dream, these animals come in as symbols of witchcraft operating against you and there is a need to deal with them. Special prayers are needed to break the influence of these systems over one's life.

Bees and hornets are some of the tools employed by these systems to bring pain and affliction.

5. Dreams of flying
    These dreams rarely appear when there is no danger or need to be lifted above attacks and even negative situations. They come to indicate that the dreamer is being lifted above any form of challenge in their life. When the dreamer wakes up, they are filled with joy and excitement because their spirit's sense the deliverance.

6. Dreams of vehicles
    These dreams represent the calling or purpose over your life depending on the type of vehicle. Please note when looking at these types of dreams the type of vehicle, the colour, as well as who is with you in that car. Are you the one driving or it is someone else? Are you able to drive or you're having difficulties? It can be a bus, plane, boat or luxury car. Different forms of vehicles have their own definitions in dreams, but they all represent purpose and calling.

7. Dreams of Being chased
    These dreams come to reveal enemies that are working in your life. Take note of who is chasing you and the location. What are your

feelings? Did you manage to flee from them? These dreams come to show you battles you're fighting and at times do not reveal strategy on how to deal with them. I will include prayers of dealing with enemies after your purpose and life in the last section of this book. If, in the dream, you have positive feelings and peace, it's a positive dream. You may have strayed away from God's purpose and being chased back towards Him.

8. Dreams of living or dead relatives
   These dreams come to indicate areas of blessing or curses that are generational. You need discernment to perceive whether this is a blessing or curse dream. This is not to say if they're dead, it's automatically a curse or if alive, it's a blessing. They're symbols of both, so there is need for wisdom. Note that it doesn't mean seeing a dead relative is always negative but one must be careful.

9. Dreams of water
   These dreams are dependent on the colour of the water and the scenery within the dream. Some of the dreams indicate the presence of God while others demonic influence. Clear water is a symbol at times of God's Spirit, while dirty water negative demonic spirits. Note that

what you're doing in the water determines the full interpretation of the dream.

10.   Dreams of dying

These dreams are not always literal but an indication of something that is passing away in an individual's life. This can be at times positive but always pray to seek clarity of interpretation to cancel if it is a direct interpretation. If it's an area that is passing away in an individual's life, it's important to note which area as well.

11.   Dreams of dogs

These dreams have parallel meanings. At one end, it's a dream of angelic help while at the other, it can be a symbol of a demonic spirit. The most common spirit that operates as a dog is a spirit of lust. The dog can also mean a friend or even a spirit of fear. Note that the colour and scenes in the dream determine interpretation.

12.   Dreams of giving birth

These dreams are a symbol of a new season that's about to manifest in an individual's life. Take note of the colours of the clothes the child would be wearing. Emotions within the dream will help you understand the new season you're about to walk into. It's different if the person is pregnant because it could be a direct dream.

13.   Dreams called nightmares
These are common with children and indicate generational enemies that need to be dealt with and cut off from having influence over your children. Stand against them in prayer and declare the freedom of your children. If it's an adult, there are deeper issues that need to be dealt with.

14.   Dreams of going through doors and gates
These dreams indicate you getting into new areas in your life and indicate promotion at times and break through into new areas of life.

15.   Dreams of taking a shower
These dreams indicate things that are being flushed out of your life and areas of deliverance. It can be from a weight of sin that had been hindering you. Allow God to help you to access the full rights of your salvation by yielding to His Spirit for your deliverance and cleansing.

16.   Dreams of clocks and watches
These dreams reveal what time it is in your life and the need for watchfulness. It's important to

note who is giving the watch or what type of watch it is.

17. Dreams of falling

These dreams indicate an area of fear. It can be something you are afraid of losing or something you are falling out of, like an area of bondage that you are being freed from.

18. Dreams of scriptural verses

These dreams indicate a message from God. Meditation of particular scriptures is important until you receive full understanding of message.

19. Dreams of going to school

These types of dreams are an indication of a test one is taking for the purpose of promotion. However, if the dreamer sees themselves in primary school, it's going back on past issues and maybe a failed test in life or things you didn't overcome and can bring back unnecessary areas of bondage. There is need for prayer for one to be freed from these attacks. But being in high school means school of the Spirit and it's positive.

20. Dreams of storms

Storms are negative, demonic, attacks over regions and nations. These usually are evil manipulations over these places. These dreams often come to people with an intercessory ministry and at times so that they can pray for that region. It can also indicate blessing if there are showers. Those that have these dreams have a lot of work in prayer and are, at times, watchmen.

21.   Dreams of teeth
There are three different types of teeth — wisdom, the eye and incisors. And when you see each falling out, it indicates an attack in the area they represent. The wisdom tooth shows the loss of wisdom or memory. Losing an eye tooth shows the loss of vision and sometimes the focus on your purpose while losing the incisors reflects the loss of ability to fight.

22.   Dreams of past relationships
These dreams indicate falling back into old habits or temptation in a particular area depending on who the person was and who they represent to you.

SECTION 3

DREAM DIRECTORY

THE following dream symbols and their definitions are from my own experiences as well as lessons from John Paul Jackson's teachings on dreams. The Dream Directory is part of his life work in the book, *Students' Manual on Dreams*.

Numbers

Numbers have some figures that may not be on the Number Chart but appear in your dreams. Let's say the year 1984 keeps appearing in your dreams. When using the number directory for numbers that don't appear on the Number Chart, you can add as the Spirit of God leads you to come up with the interpretation. Try it on the year you were born and see the purpose you were born for using the Number Directory. Let's look at 1984 together; 1+9+8+4=22. If you notice, the number 22 is not on the Number Chart below, so we add again; 2+2= 4. Then 4 becomes the purpose why this individual was born for. Let's look at the numbers individually. 1 is God/beginning, 9 is fruitful/evangelist/judgement, 8 is new beginning/teacher and 4 is influence on all spheres of the world/rule.

For individual numbers that are on the chart, it's always easier, but it gets complicated with bigger numbers. But the more you use the chart, the easier it becomes.

1– God, Beginning, New beginning (Gen 1:1; Eph. 4:4-6; Jn. 10:30; Jn. 17:21-22)

2 – Multiplication/division/ union/ confirmation/ testimony/ witness (Gen 2:23-24; Matt 18:16; 1Kings 3:24-25; Gen 1:7-8)

3 – Godhead (Triune God)/Divine Completeness/perfection/resurrection/restoration (Mt 12:40; Mt 28:19; Ezek. 14:14-18)

4 – God's creative works/ rule or to reign/influence/ helpers /influence in all spheres of the world (Gen 1:14-19)

5 - Grace/redemption/ fivefold ministry (Eph. 4:11; Gen 1:20-23)

6 - Man, beast, Satan (Gen 1:26-27)

7 - Perfection/completion/Rest/Blessing (Gen 2:1-3; Rev 10:7; Rev 16:17; Deut. 15:1-2)

8 – New Beginnings (Teacher) (Gen 17:12; Lk 2:21-23; 1Pet 3:20)

9 -Judgment (Evangelist)/ finality / fullness/Harvest (Gal 5:22-23; 1Cor.12:8-10;

10- Journey/ Wilderness/ law/ government/ responsibility (Pastor) (Ex 34:28)

11 – Transition (Prophet) (Dan 7:24; Gen 32:22)

12 – Government/apostolic fullness (Apostle) (Lk 6:12-13; Mt 19:28)

13 – Rebellion/ backsliding/ apostasy/ death (Gen14:4; 1 Kings 11:6)

14 – Double anointing (Mt 1:17)

15 – Reprieve/ mercy / perfect Grace (Lev 23:34-35; Ester 9:20-22)

16 – Established beginnings/ love (1Cor 13:4-8)

17 – Election/Immaturity/ Transition/ Victory (Gen 47:28)

25 – Begin ministry training, Perfection

30 – Begin ministry (Num 4:3-4; Gen 41:46; 2Sam 5:4)

111 – My Beloved Son

666 – Full lawlessness, anti-Christ

888 – Resurrection

10,000 – Maturity

Colour Chart

Each colour is unique and at times in a dream, the dreamer usually does not focus on the colour, which stops one from receiving full interpretation of the dream. At times, if one misses the colour, they may miss the full meaning of the dream. But note that there are dreams in which colours are elusive, so it's important to remember the colour. There are also dreams that don't have colour.

- Amber: God's glory, the brightness of His Presence, grace, purity, holiness, anointing of fire, coming together, protection
- Amethyst: Dreams, prophetic, modesty, sobriety
- Black: Fear of the Lord, priesthood, prophetic, beauty, abundance, moved with passion, protective, calamity, sin, darkness, sorrow, worldliness, midnight hour, physical affliction, enemy, wickedness, demonic
- Blue: Spirit of might, revelation, blessing, heaven, healing, justice, goodwill, celestial/heavenly power, spiritual dominance, heaven-bestowed rulership, unimpeded growth, unlimited potential, eternity's government, God's appearance, faith, Communion with God, winter, depression, sorrow, anxiety, isolation
- Bronze: fortification, primitive, unrefined, harlotry, demotion, sin, Forgiveness
- Brown: compassion, pastor, humility, repentant, born again, humanity, devotion, earth, richness, self-effort, dead, sacrifice
- Gold: Glory, knowledge, praise, truth, holiness, favour, eternal life, kingship, divine nature of Jesus, man's spirit, royalty and transcendence, opulent wealth and spiritual power, refinement of the spirit, idolatry, defilement, greed.

- Grey: Honour, dignity, splendour, wisdom, glory, humility, maturity, dullness
- Green: Spirit of counsel, new life, prosperity, healing, sonship, victory, wealth, money, youth, renewal, peace, colour of prophet, divine activity, throne room, inexperienced, immature, pride, jealousy
- Ivory: Quiet
- Magenta: The Father's heart, unconditional love, emotions, joy, judgment, warning, fear, hate
- Maroon: Wild, untamed, untrained, novice, youthfulness.
- Orange: Spirit of wisdom, perseverance, strength, power, energy, harvest, change of season, fire, tried and proven, persecution, rebellion, witchcraft, danger
- Pink: Femininity, innocence, chaste, purity, feminine, female
- Rebellion, immoral, flesh, priesthood during prayer/sacrifice, prophetic, morning
- Purple: spirit of discernment, authority, kingship, royalty, majestic, royal priesthood, apostle, prince, Princess, queen, dishonesty, Jezebel, false authority.
- Violet: The Spirit of the Fear of the Lord, mental clarity, emotions
- Indigo: Spirit of knowledge, authority to heal, internal issues, mental disorder, pain

- Red: The Spirit of the Lord, wisdom, power, prophetic anointing, life, blood atonement, honour, courage, royalty in warfare, colour of conquered land, prayer, evangelist, sin, death
- Silver: Wisdom, the soul and its spiritual sphere, prosperity, opportunity for fortune, leadership, redemption, grace, refining process, salvation, mercy, legalism, slavery, betrayal
- White: Love, Holy Spirit, angels, purity, light, holiness, righteousness, Bride of Christ, triumph, victory in conflict, success, religious spirit, witchcraft, unimaginative
- Yellow: Family, wealth, spirit of understanding, hope, light, celebration, renewed mind, gift of God, soul, Fear, coward, sissy, illness, hazards, dishonesty, intellectual pride

Animal Symbols

Bat – witchcraft, wavering, fear.

Bear – judgment, strength; an evil spirit that wants something you have

Polar Bear – religious spirit

Bird – symbol of spirits, good or evil
Bull – persecution, spiritual warfare, opposition, accusation, slander, threat, economic increase

Camel – long journey, endurance, preparedness

Cat – self-willed, untrainable, predator, unclean spirit, bewitching charm, stealthy, sneaky, deception

Black Cat – witchcraft

White Cat – spiritualist (*sangoma* and occultic churches)

Cheetah – swift, fast, predator, danger, and can be play on word for "Cheater" (spirit of lust, temptation).
Chicken – Fear, cowardliness; hen can be protection, gossip, motherhood; rooster can be boasting, bragging, proud; chick can be defenceless, innocent.

Crab – not easy to approach

Crow (raven) – confusion, outspoken, operating in envy or strife, hateful, unclean, God's minister of justice or provision

Crocodile: Ancient, evil out of the past, danger, destruction, evil spirit, or slander and gossip (big mouth), aggression

Cow – subsistence, prosperity, idol and idolatry

Deer – Graceful, swift, sure-footed, agile, timid

Dog – spirit of lust, spirit of fear, unbelievers, religious hypocrites, loyalty, friendship, faithfulness

Donkey – gentle strength, burden bearer, negative (stubborn, delay, unproductive).

Dove – Holy Spirit

Dragon – Satan

Dinosaur – old stronghold, demonic, danger from the past (generational stronghold)

Eagle – prophetic, prophetic calling

Elephant – Invincible or thick skinned, not easily offended, powerful, large, having great impact, storing memory, old memory, long pregnancy

Fish – souls of men

Fox – cunning, evil men, sly, sneaky, something that steals from you

Frog – Spirit of Lust.

Goat – No discernment, positive: prosperity in some cultures, pride, boastful.

Horse – Power, strength, conquest

Leopard – swiftness, sometimes associated with vengeance, predator, danger

Lion – Jesus ("Lion of the tribe of Judah"), royalty and kingship, bravery, confidence, Satan seeking to destroy

Lobster – not easy to approach

Mice – Devourer, curse, plague, timid

Mole – spiritual blindness, hidden

Monkey – foolishness, clinging, mischief, dishonesty, addiction Mountain Lion – enemy, predator of your soul
Owl – witchcraft, messenger of Satin, occultic.

Octopus – Jezebel Spirit because of the tentacles Ox - slow change, subsistence

Black Panther – high level witchcraft, demonic activity, works in darkness

Pig – Ignorance, hypocrisy, religious unbelievers, unclean people, selfish, gluttonous, vicious, vengeful

Ram – Sacrifice

Rat – (feeds on garbage or impurities), unclean spirit, invader raven – evil, Satan, unexpected helpers (may lead to trouble at the end), thieves.

Serpent – Satan and evil spirits

Sheep – People of God, innocent, vulnerable, humility, submission, sacrifice

Skunk – stench, smell, messy situation, unforgiveness, bitterness, bad attitude

Sloth – Slow moving, easy prey, vulnerable

Snake – Deception, lies, Satan, unforgiveness, bitterness
- White Snake – Spirit of religion, occult
- Yellow snake – blood related spirits
- Black snake – family altar/ idol

Sparrow – Small value but precious

Tiger – Danger, powerful minister (both good and evil), soul power

Tortoise – Slow moving, slow change, steady, old way of doing something, wise Whale – Big impact in the things of the Spirit

Wolf – Satan and evil, false ministries and false teachers

Insects

Ant –team work, hard workers, organised assault, sick irritation
Bee/hornet- painful, strong demonic attack

Butterfly – Freedom, flighty, fragile temporary glory, transformation

Flies – Evil spirits, filth of Satan's kingdom (Beelzebub is "Lord of the flies"), live on dead things, occultic

Grasshopper – destruction

Moth – symbol of destruction

Roach – Infestation, unclean spirits, hidden sin

Scorpion – Evil spirits, evil men, pinch of pain

Spider – occultic attack, witchcraft

Spider Web – place of demonic attack, ensnaring, a trap

Mopani worm – transition, restoration of health and lost glory, destruction of ability to make wealth

Buildings and Places

Note the size and purpose of the building.

Hut – family, coming together, unity, provision, generational issues.

Kitchen hut – provision, coming together

Bedroom hut – intimacy, issues that date back to your childhood.

House – a ministry, a church, a personal life situation, your life or family. When you dream about a previous home, what happened in that house is important (anything that started when you where there).

Buying, or living in, the house of a known person in the ministry – God has a similar call on your life.

Two-story house – double anointing

Castle – authority, fortress, royal residence

Barn/warehouse – a place of provision and storage

Mall – marketplace, provision for all needs in 1 place. Negative – self centeredness, materialism

Stadium – place of tremendous impact

School, Classroom – Training period, a place of teaching; a ministry with teaching anointing

Elevator – rising or descending of anointing

Staircase – up or down in the spirit (anointing). It can speak of portals or foundations in relation to important foundational issues

High-rise buildings – high spiritual calling or high spiritual perspective

Hotel – transition, temporary, place to relax or receive

Country General Store – provision, basics, staples

Mobile home – temporary place and condition, It is going to move or can move. It can represent poverty

Tent – temporary place of rest. Meeting place with God Amphitheatre – something is going to be magnified.

Theatre – going to be shown something, or visibility is increasing

Windows – vision, letting light in, ideas and knowledge.

Atrium – light and growth from heaven

Garden – love, intimacy, growth

Front porch – vision or future

Back porch – history or past

Hallway – transition that is usually direct or without deviation

Hospital – place of healing

Garage – place to rest and refresh, place of protection, a covering for ministries

Auto repair shop – ministry restoration, renewal and repair

Gas station – to receive power

Office building – getting things accomplished, depending on what's in the building
Roof – spiritual covering, marital cover

Shack – poverty

Farm – place of provision

Rooms in a House

Bathroom – place of deliverance, sign of spiritual toxins removed

Bathroom in full view – humbling season: others aware of deliverance.

Kitchen – preparing spiritual food, provision

Restaurant kitchen – greater influence or impact

Dining Room/Eating – partaking of spiritual food, fellowship

Attic – History, past issues, family history

Basement – hidden issues, foundation, basics

Bedroom – intimacy and rest.
Sitting room – family, relationships

Directions

East – Beginning: Law (therefore blessed or cursed); birth; first. Gen11:2; Job 38:24

North – Spiritual: Judgment; heaven; spiritual warfare (as in "taking your inheritance"). Prov 25:23; Jer. 1:13-14.

South – Natural: Sin; world; temptation; trial; flesh; corruption; deception. Josh. 10:40, Job 37:9.

West – End: Grace; death; last; conformed. Exod. 10:19; Luke 12:54.

Right – Natural; Authority; power; the strength of man (flesh) or the power of God revealed through man; accepted. (Right Turn = natural change). Matt 5:29a, 30a; 1Peter 3:22

Left – Spiritual: Weakness (of man), and therefore God's strength or ability; rejected. (Left Turn = spiritual change). Judges 3:20-21; 2 Cor. 12:9, 10.

Back – Past: As in BACKYARD or BACKDOOR. Previous event or experience (good or evil); that which is behind (in time – for example, past sins or the sins of forefathers); unaware; unsuspecting; hidden; memory. Gen. 22:13; Josh. 8:4.

Front – Future or Now: (as in FRONT YARD) in the presence of; prophecy; immediate; current. Gen.6:11; Rev.1:19.

Weather

Storms – look at the colour. Light in colour can be from God. Dark can be trouble from the enemy. Turbulent times, judgment

Tornadoes – winds of change (negative or positive depending on the colour of the tornadoes). Destructive times coming, judgment, drastic change, danger

Wind – Positive: Holy Spirit; Negative: adversity

Rain – Blessing, cleansing (clear rain), from enemy (dirty rain)

Earthquake – judgment or shaking

Snow – Blessing, refreshing, righteousness, purity

Blizzard – inability to see, storm with the purpose of blinding you

Body Parts

Thigh – faith

Nose – discernment

Hand – relationship, healing

Arm – strength, faith

Elbow and Enkol - mobility, strength

Teeth – wisdom, comprehension, understanding

Eye Teeth – revelatory understanding

Wisdom teeth – ability to act in wisdom

Immobilized Body Parts – some sort of spiritual hindrance probably under demonic attack

Beard- Maturity

Hair – wisdom and anointing

Bald Head – lacking wisdom

Nakedness – transparency, humility, humbling season,
Neck – Negative: stiff necked or stubborn. Positive: support or strength

Side – relationship, friendship

Fingers

- Thumb – apostolic
- Pointer – prophetic
- Middle – evangelistic
- Ring – pastor
- Pinky – teaching

Other Symbols

Pregnancy – in process of reproducing, preparatory stage, the promise of God, the Word of God as seed, prophetic word, desire, anticipation, expectancy, filled with the purposes of God that are preparing to come forth.

Miscarriage – to lose something at the preparatory stage, whether good or bad, plans aborted.

Television – spiritual sight and understanding, entertainment, fleshly cravings and desires, dull spirit

Money – gain or loss of favour negative – greed

Check – favour

Credit Card – attempting to walk in something that you don't have yet; debt; lack of trust

Trees – leaders, mature believers, steady

Flying – call or ability of move in the higher things of God, understanding into the spirit realm of God

Life seasons – may include former places you have been/lived, and/or former schools, tests, jobs, something significant about that season

Kiss – Coming into agreement, covenant, seductive process, enticement, deception or betrayal, betrayal from a trusted friend.

Gate – spiritual authority, entrance point for good or evil

Key – spiritual authority

Weapons and Objects

Knife – Brutal attack or gossip; if you are holding it, than form of protection Sword – Word of God, further reaching, authority

Gun – Spiritual authority good or bad, spiritual attack Dart – Curses, demonic attack, Positive – accuracy

Arrow – negative: accusation from the enemy, Positive: Blessing of children, Focused message, "shooting an arrow" with your life

Shield – Faith, protection, God's truth, faith in God

Spear – close confrontation.

Crown – symbol of authority, Seal of Power, Jesus Christ, to reign, to be honoured

Clothing

Coat – Mantle/anointing

Swimwear – Ability to move in the Spirit

Speedo – to move fast in the spirit

Shorts – a walk or calling that is partially fulfilled

Bathrobe – Coming out of a place of cleansing

Pyjamas – spiritual slumber

Cultural clothing – Going back to principals and truths you were raised with, calling to another country or intercession for a particular country or ethnic group

Wedding Dress – Covenant or deep relationship

Shoes – Gospel of peace

Clothing that doesn't fit – Walking in something you're not called to

Tattered Clothing – Mantle/anointing not being taken care of.

Transport

Airplane – able to go to heights in the Spirit (prophetic); Can relate to the church, ministry or corporation; Size and type of plane correlates to interpretation

Automobile – personal ministry, your destiny or life.

Convertible – open heaven in your personal ministry or job

Bus – church or ministry

Truck – ability to transport or deliver

Semi-truck – transporting amounts

Tow Truck – ministry of helps or gathering the wounded

Fire Truck – rescue, putting out fires of destruction

Moving Van – transition, change

Tractor – slow power, may speak about need to plough

Bicycle – Individual ministry or calling requiring perseverance

Motorcycle – fast, powerful, manoeuvrable

Armoured Car – protection of God, caution attack coming

Taxi Cab – a shepherd or hireling for someone (driving). Paying the price to get where you are going (passenger)

Stagecoach – rough, difficult ride

Scotch cart – prosperity, mobility, delay if donkey-driven

Rollercoaster – Positive – a wild ride that God is directing, exciting, but temporary

Negative – A path of destruction that has the appearance of exciting at first

Limousine – being taken to your destiny in style. Negative – materialism

Train – a movement of God

Coal car – on track, being directed by the Lord

Hang glider – going somewhere in the Spirit; Being driven by the wind of the spirit Mini Van – family

Ocean liner – impacting large numbers of people

Tugboat – providing assistance, ministry of helps

Sailboats – powered by wind of the Spirit

Riverboat – Slow, but impacting many people

Speedboat – fast, exciting, power in the Spirit

Submarine – undercover and active, not seen by many

Subway – undercover and active, but not seen by many

Helicopter – mobile, flexible, able to get in Spirit quickly
Chariot – major spiritual encounter

Spaceship – to the outer limits spiritually speaking
People

Baby – New ministry or responsibility that has recently been birthed. New beginning, new idea, dependent, helpless, innocent, sin

Chief – authority figure, influence in a particular community. Your case shall be heard; your voice will be heard

Twins – double blessing/anointing

Negative – double trouble

Mob – false accusation, occultic man gathering against you

Harlot / Prostitute – a tempting situation; something that appeals to your flesh; worldly desire; a demon

Hijacker – enemy wanting to take control of you or a situation; positive – God taking control Husband – Jesus Christ, actual person

Lawyer – Jesus Christ (our advocate); the accuser of the brethren (Satan); pertaining to legalism; mediator

Prisoner – a lost soul

Shepherd – Jesus Christ, God; leader, good or bad; selfless person, protector

Carpenter – Jesus, someone who makes or mends things, a preacher Bride – Christ's church, Covenant or relationship

Giant – Godly men, strong, conquer, demons, defilement
Policemen – Authority for good or evil, protector, spiritual authority

Food Items

Apples – spiritual fruit, temptation, something precious like the apple of God's eyes

Tomato – Kindness, the heart of God, big hearted, very generous

Strawberries – goodness, excellence in nature and virtue, healing, sweet and very humble

Lemons – sour, a poor sport

Pears – long life, enduring much without complaining

Manna – God's miraculous provision, coming directly from God, glory of God, bread of life.

Bread – Jesus Christ, bread of life, Word of God, source of nourishment, God's provision

Wine – working of the Spirit of God, Move of God, Negative – drunkenness, love of the world

Meat – something meant for the spiritually mature, depth in God's word

Milk – Good nourishment, elementary teaching Water – Holy Spirit, refreshing, Word of God

Eggs – promise of God. Prayers yet to be fulfilled. Something that has not yet "hatched" or come into being.

Grapes – Fruitfulness, success in life, fruit of the vine, evidence of being connected to Christ

Honey – Sweet, strength, wisdom, Spirit of God, abiding anointing, sweet Word of our Lord, the best of the land, abundance

SECTION 4

DREAMS AND WARFARE

THE king woke up and he was restless. The dream had chased away peace from his heart and the peace could only be restored when he understood what the interpretation of the dream was. He had been a great general and men trembled at the sight of him. Yet a single dream brought so much fear to his heart. No matter what tittle or rank a dream always vexes the soul if not understood.

A decree went out: all the wise man would be killed if they could not remind the king his dream. The wise man and magicians that where at times his most trusted adviser could not remind him his dream and provide its interpretation.

Daniel asked for more time to look at the dream. But the king could not afford it because the dream had caused him too much despair.

It is often the nature of dreams to trouble the dreamer. Imagine a king lost peace because of a dream! The only way he regained the rest was when he received the interpretation. Many have felt like this especially if the dreams seem to be an unbreakable cycle.

How do you break demonic cycles in dreams if they keep persisting? A young lady would relate me how she did not find pleasure in sleep anymore because of demonic attacks.

Dream 1

My wife in a dream saw a cat that had white and black spots. She said she killed the cat and when we woke up in the morning she told me the story. To my surprise by our door outside was the cat that she had described to me that she had dreamt of. Imagine if the cat had victory in the dream. She could have lost her life.

These dreams can bring death to the dreamer and the only way to deal with them is to build capacity in the word and in prayer. The more you feed on the word the greater your capacity to deal with these attacks. Most attacks like these individuals wake up dead. So my wife by grace had capacity to deal with this spirit of witchcraft sent against her.

If she did not have capacity in the word to deal with the cat she would have died. Before you have victory in dreams build capacity when you're awake. Many never wake up because they don't have the Word and have not built capacity through the Word.

Most of the attacks that happen in dreams affect those that have not trained themselves in the natural.

Dream 2

A woman started having negative sexual dreams with her in-law after she got married and the in-law would force himself on her in her dreams. During marriage, the woman had also been married off to the family idol and she was not aware of it. The only way out was to deal with this idol against her. This dream is an attack that one deals with in the Word and prayer by standing against this idol. Read prayers on the blood in this section.

Dream 3

I remember a dream that a woman in South Africa sent me. In the dream, she saw herself brushing her teeth using black pepper as tooth paste. As I read the dream, the Lord showed me how there was a problem with ashma within her family and how others would face breathing challenges because of overweight. She had to deal with this situation through prayers but first she had to receive revelation of her situation. When you understand your dream it is easier to pray.

How to have Victory in Your Dreams

When dealing with attacks in a dream, you need to understand the weapons you have been given to fight spiritual wars with. The blood of Jesus Christ is a weapon. Pastor Chris Oyakhilome, in the book, *The Promised Land*, says, "it's not fully effective to shout 'I plead the blood of Jesus because to plead one must have evidence'. In the New Testament, we have the blood of Jesus which speaks better things than that of Abel yet you need an understanding of how to approach the courts of heaven with the evidence of the blood to plead your case."

Whenever you experience an attack in a dream, learn to bring the enemy before the courts of heaven with the evidence of the blood through communion. In communion, you have legality to say, with that communion, you declare and plead over whatever situation or Dream you need to deal with.

Prayers of the Blood in Communion

I take this communion and bring the host of heaven to remembrance of the power of the cross that set me free.

I declare I am free from sexual attacks in my dreams

I declare I am free from serpents sent against me in my dreams

I declare devil you have no right over me and my family

I declare my enemies will not continue to accuse me in my dreams.

I, through this communion, declare the blood of Jesus is louder than the voice of my enemies.

Take note that whenever you plead the blood, bring fourth evidence through the Holy Communion and lay charges against your enemies as you create prayers that speak to your situation.

Weapons of Warfare in Dreams

The Bible declares every knee in heaven and on earth shall bow to the name of Jesus. As long as anything has a name, it has to bow. Demonic agents in dreams have no option but to bow.

Prayers raised to bring down altars and agents of the devil in your dreams.

I declare and decree any arrow sent against me in the night as
I sleep return back to sender in Jesus name

I declare by fire no altar shall stand against me in my dream in Jesus' name

Every snake and demonic spirit is paralysed in Jesus' name
I can't be bond and opressed by sexual demons in Jesus' name
No blood line spirit has power over me in Jesus' name

I declare I am hidden with Christ in God, therefore devils have no access to me in Jesus' name

These are just prayer patterns to deal with any system that has been fighting you in your dreams and can be applied differently to any situation.

Conclusion

The more faithful you are, the more your dreams become clearer. I have observed that dreams become easier to understand when you learn to steward every dream you are given. Yes, Jesus spoke in parables to some but to His disciples he spoke directly. God spoke Moses as a man speaks to his friend. But to grow to this level learn to value and steward his voice.

Contact the writer

+27610286350
mtandwah@gmail.com.

Like our page, Humphrey Mtandwa

 Books by Humphrey Mtandwa

Enoch Generation
Truthfulness
Theophany
My Release

Made in United States
Troutdale, OR
10/20/2023